Writing
Yellow Pages

for Students and Teachers

Revised Edition

from the Kids' Stuff™ People

Incentive Publications, Inc.
Nashville, Tennessee

Special acknowledgement is accorded to

- *Marjorie Frank for compiling and organizing
  the materials included in this publication*

- *Susan Eaddy for the cover art*

- *Jean K. Signor, Editor*

ISBN 0-86530-561-7
Library of Congress Control Number: 2001094390

PRINTED IN THE UNITED STATES OF AMERICA
www.incentivepublications.com

Table of Contents

Writing Ideas

WRITING SKILLS CHECKLIST

EFFECTIVE WORD USE

_____ Recognize and choose precise words for accurate meaning and interest

_____ Recognize and choose interesting, effective words for strengthening written pieces

_____ Identify and avoid over-used words or clichés

_____ Recognize and choose active rather than inactive words and phrases

_____ Identify and select words that help to create certain moods

_____ Identify sentences with word arrangements that produce clarity, rhythm, and flow

_____ Arrange words in sentences in a manner that makes the meaning clear

_____ Arrange words in sentences to give an interesting rhythm and smooth flow

_____ Identify words or phrases that are repetitive or unnecessary in a written passage

_____ Identify words or phrases that suggest the author's bias

_____ Recognize and choose words and phrases that produce strong sensory images; identify the sense to which the writing appeals

RECOGNITION OF FORMS & TECHNIQUES

_____ Identify examples and uses of expository, descriptive, persuasive, and imaginative writing

_____ Recognize passages in which varied sentence structure and length makes the writing interesting and effective

_____ Distinguish between poetry and prose; identify characteristics of each

_____ Identify definitions or characteristics of different forms of writing

_____ Identify use of writing techniques and literary devices (puns, similes, metaphors, idioms, alliteration, personification, hyperbole, onomatopoeia)

_____ Identify good use of details to support and enhance an idea

_____ Identify the point of view from which a passage was written

_____ Recognize writing in which form, style, or content appeals to a specific audience

_____ Recognize writing in which form, style, or content fits a certain purpose for the writing

_____ Identify specific uses of literary techniques in a passage

_____ Identify ways a writer uses words for a particular purpose

_____ Recognize sensory appeal in a passage

EFFECTIVE USE OF FORMS & TECHNIQUES

_____ Show ability to produce a variety of kinds of writing: expository, descriptive, persuasive, and imaginative writing

_____ Use sentences of varying structure and length

_____ Show ability to use writing techniques and literary devices (puns, similes, metaphors, idioms, alliteration, personification, hyperbole, onomatopoeia)

_____ Include interesting, relevant details to support and enhance an idea

_____ Adapt form, style, and content appropriately for appeal to a specific audience

_____ Adapt form, style, and content appropriately for the purpose of the writing

_____ Show appropriate word choice for the purpose and audience

_____ Include fresh, specific, varied, and colorful words in written pieces

_____ Include dialogue in the text, where effective and appropriate

_____ Show ability to engage the audience and convey personal commitment (voice) to the writing

_____ Develop experience writing in a variety of forms such as these: titles, articles, character studies, stories, poems, myths, essays, advertisements, arguments, explanations, imaginary tales, narrations, etc.

CONTENT & ORGANIZATION

_____ Create written pieces that show completeness and clear organization

_____ State main ideas and purposes clearly

_____ Use sufficient and relevant details and examples to support a main idea

_____ Combine ideas and details in a way that flows smoothly

_____ Combine ideas and details in a way that develops meaning clearly

_____ Combine ideas and details in a sensible sequence

_____ Contribute ideas that have freshness

_____ Create strong titles for written pieces

_____ Create strong, attention-getting beginnings

_____ Create strong, effective endings or conclusions

_____ Show ability to use a variety of resources when gathering ideas or facts for writing

EDITING*

_____ Show ability to give thoughtful and constructive responses to others' writing

_____ Recognize and replace overused, ordinary, or inactive words and phrases

_____ Revise sentences for clarity, rhythm, and flow

_____ Rearrange ideas or lines for proper sequence, better meaning, or better flow

_____ Eliminate excess or repetitive words or ideas in sentences

_____ Eliminate repetitive unrelated ideas in passages

_____ Vary lengths of sentences for smoothness or effectiveness in conveying meaning

_____ Improve weak beginnings

_____ Improve weak endings or conclusions

_____ Replace weak or imprecise titles

_____ Strengthen a passage by adding dialogue, or by changing existing text to dialogue

_____ Revise writing for accuracy in capitalization and punctuation (including quotations)

_____ Revise writing for spelling accuracy

_____ Revise writing for correct use of grammatical construction

WRITING PROCESS

_____ Show ability to participate in each part of the writing process

_____ Take part in motivational activities that stimulate ideas

_____ Actively and fluently collect ideas, words, and phrases for writing

_____ Organize a rough draft using collected ideas

_____ Examine own writing for technique, effectiveness, and organization

_____ Examine and respond to others' writing appropriately and constructively

_____ Use responses and observations to make revisions in own writing

_____ Review own writing carefully for correctness in conventions

_____ Prepare a polished, finished piece after reviewing for revision needs

_____ Take part in sharing, presenting, or publishing finished products

*See also: Editor's Guides on pages 58 and 59

WRITING FOR EVERYDAY LIVING

Gain experience with writing these and other frequently-needed forms

Letter Writing

____ Friendly letters

____ Social notes

____ Business letters

____ Invitations

____ Envelopes

Informational and Instructional Writing

____ Graphs and diagrams

____ Signs and posters

____ Basic informational paragraphs

____ Summaries of information

____ Procedural directions

____ Geographical directions

Informational Forms

____ Identification and registration

____ Applications

____ Contracts

____ Order blanks

Organizing and Recording Factual Data

____ Record keeping and inventories

____ Note-taking

____ Memos

____ Biographies

____ Journals and diaries

____ Lists

____ Ads

____ Reports

THINGS TO WRITE

A

advertisements
advice columns
allegories
anecdotes
announcements
answers
anthems
apologies
assumptions
autobiographies
awards

B

ballads
beauty tips
bedtime stories
beginnings
billboards
biographies
blurbs
books
book jackets
book reviews
brochures
bulletins
bumper stickers

C

calendar quips
campaign speeches
captions
cartoons
catalog entries
CD covers
cereal boxes
certificates
character sketches
church bulletins
community bulletins
cinquains
clues
codes
comic strips
commercials
comparisons

complaints
constitutions
contracts
contrasts
conundrums
conversations
couplets
critiques
crossword puzzle clues
cumulative stories

D

definitions
descriptions
dialogues
diamantes
diaries
diets
directions
directories
documents
doubletalk
dramas
dream scripts

E

editorials
e-mails
encyclopedia entries
epilogues
epitaphs
endings
essays
evaluations
exaggerations
exclamations
explanations

F

fables
fairy tales
fantasies
fashion show scripts
feature articles
folklore
free verse

G

gags
game rules
good news/bad news
gossip
graffiti
greeting cards
grocery lists

H

haiku
headlines
health tips
horoscopes
"how-to" booklets
"how-NOT-to" booklets
hymns

I

impromptu speeches
indexes
inquiries
interviews
introductions
invitations

J

jingles
job applications
job descriptions
jokes
journals
jump rope rhymes

L

legends
letters
limericks
lists
love notes
luscious words
lyrics

M

magazines
malapropisms
marquee notices
memories
memos
menus
metaphors
minutes
monologues
movie reviews
mysteries
myths

N

newscasts
news flashes
newspapers
nonsense
notes
novels
nursery rhymes

O

obituaries
observations
odes
opinions

P

palindromes
pamphlets
parodies
party tips
persuasive letters
phrases
plays
poems
post cards
post scripts
posters
prayers
predictions
problems
problem solutions
product descriptions
programs

profound sayings
prologues
propaganda
proposals
protest letters
proverbs
puns
puppet shows
puzzles

Q

questions
questionnaires
quips
quizzes
quotations

R

reactions
real estate notices
rebuttals
recipes
remedies
reports
requests
Requiems
resumes
reviews
rhymes
riddles

S

sale notices
sales pitches
satires
sayings
schedules
science fiction
secrets
self-portraits
sentences
sequels
serialized stories
sermons
signs
silly sayings
skywriting messages
slogans

songs
sonnets
speeches
spoofs
spooky stories
spoonerisms
sports accounts
stories
summaries
superstitions

T

TV commercials
TV guides
TV scripts
tall tales
telegrams
telephone directory
textbooks
thank you notes
theater programs
travel posters
titles
tongue twisters
travel brochures
tributes
trivia

V

vignettes
vitae

W

want ads
wanted posters
warnings
weather forecasts
weather reports
web pages
wills
wise sayings
wishes
words

Y

yarns
yellow pages

THINGS TO WRITE ON

stationery, tablets, pads, notebooks
computers
acetate
e-mail
file folders
fabric
index cards
grocery sacks, shopping bags
gift bags
paper towels
web pages
kites
gift-wrap paper
canvas
cardboard, poster board, tagboard
construction paper
tissue paper
cakes & cookies
calculator paper
old window shades
plastic tablecloths
hats
T-shirts
old lamp shades
paper plates and cups
stones and rocks
leaves
wooden spoons
wood strips, shingles
bricks and concrete blocks
masking or packing tape
*hands and feet
*bodies
*bathtubs
*sinks
*mirrors
*windows
*cookie sheets
*pot lids
*sidewalks, streets
*drinking glasses
*sunglasses
*dust pans
*plastic plates, cups, and glasses
*plastic table tops
*countertops
*glass table tops
*refrigerator doors

*(*Be sure to write on these only with permission, and use only water-soluble writing materials!)*

THINGS TO WRITE WITH

pencils
pens
chalk
computers
paint
soap
shoe polish
shaving cream
toothpaste
feathers
lipstick
cake frosting
yarn or twine
glue
liquid paper *(white-out™)*
mud
old wallpaper
fingers of a glove
boxes
twigs and sticks
paintbrushes
sponges
ribbon
string
fingers and toes
shells
stones
syrup
pudding
salt or sand
buttons
rope
beans
seeds
cereal
nails and tacks
rags and cotton balls
letters cut from magazines, newspapers,
    bulletins, and brochures
needle and thread
words cut from greeting cards
pasta or dried beans *(with glue)*
pretzel sticks
toothpicks or Q-tips™
whipped cream
crayons
felt markers
cheese *(the kind that squirts out of a can)*

THINGS TO WRITE ABOUT

Write about some of these things. The writing can be real or imaginary, serious or silly, factual or fictitious, impartial or biased.

Choose any form that fits your topic. (See pages 11 and 12 for many choices.)

Let these topics inspire you to think about other good topics for writing.

adventures — real or imaginary, any kind, anywhere, and any time in history or the future

annoyances — things that anger, bother, mildly disturb, or disappoint you

art — any kind of work of art, including those that YOU create

beliefs — yours or someone else's . . . What are they? Why are they believed?

books — any book, whether you like it or not.

changes — why things have, might, did not, or should change

current events — whatever is *(or is not)* in the news, in the world or in your neighborhood

dreams — daydreams or nighttime dreams

entertainment — any show, commercial, program, or other kind of performance

families — interesting relatives, their antics, relationships, and influences on each other

fantasies — all that good stuff that probably cannot happen, but just maybe . . .

feelings — joy, jealousy, surprise, fury, hurt, frustration, or any other human feeling

food — all that tempting, enticing, delicious, fun, luscious, or disgusting stuff

friends — their lives, their characteristics, their relationships, their activities

the future — adventures, possibilities, lifestyles, technology that might be

good deeds — touching, surprising, or unnoticed good things people do

hobbies — yours or the surprising hobbies of others

holidays — what's great *(or not great)* about any holiday; or which holidays should be invented

hot issues — topics out there that are capturing the passions of people, right now!

imaginary creatures — such as ghosts, goblins, leprechauns, trolls, elves, gnomes

land formations — mountains, hills, valleys, canyons, caves, gorges, canals, plateaus

manners — admirable behavior, bad behavior, or in between

the media — what it does *(or does not)* do, what is good, bad, harmful, enriching, controlling, etc.

money — what it does, how to save or spend or earn it, how to get rid of its influence

music — songs, lyrics, groups, influences

mysteries — anything that you cannot quite explain or understand

myths — tales of wormholes, the Bermuda Triangle, the Loch Ness Monster, Bigfoot, the abominable snowman, ghost ships, or other mythical places, creatures, or occurrences

natural disasters — tornadoes, cyclones, black holes, earthquakes, floods, fires, hurricanes

outdoors — wide-open spaces—the thrills, adventures, dangers

outer space — watching it, wondering about it, traveling in it

the past — fascinating, amazing, or surprising things that happened— real or imaginary

people — ordinary or extraordinary folks and their interesting or quirky characteristics

places — interesting or unusual, real or imaginary *(why we should or should NOT visit them)*

politics — public officials, elections, issues, candidates, or strange happenings

problems — any kind of a situation, dilemma, or trouble that needs solving

propaganda — all the influences that are out there, subtly trying to control your mind and behavior

questions — confusions, wonderings, or other unanswered situations

science or technology — gadgets, inventions, or gismos and how they work

school — anything that is ripe for a story, opinion, celebration, joke, complaint, or news flash

social events — teams, meetings, parties, or any other gatherings—real or fictitious

someone else's life — a biography of part or all of the life of someone interesting to you

sports — tales that need to be told about any sporting event or athlete *(any age)*

a town, country, or city — any place that has a fascinating story waiting to be told

tragedies — things that you wish had never happened

travel — adventures unlimited around, beneath, or above the earth, or into imaginary places

the unknown — questions, adventures, explanations, or explorations of anything unknown

water — things that happen in rushing rivers, dangerous waterfalls, wild oceans, and calm lakes

weather — hail, sleet, blizzards, tornados, deep fogs, thunderstorms, and such

your life — the story of all or part of your very own life

IDEAS FOR IMPROVING WORD USE

- These ideas will help writers learn new words, and use words that are more powerful, interesting, precise, and effective in their written work.

- Go on scavenger hunts for good words. Look in magazines, stories, textbooks, advertisements, and everything you read.

- Keep word lists. Build a notebook that contains all kinds of good words for writing. *(See page 18 for great ideas on some kinds of words to collect.)*

- Try to learn a new word each week. Write the word on your calendar, and try to use it at least twice every day in the week.

- Read advertisements and product descriptions in magazines, on cereal boxes, and on posters. Listen to advertisements on TV and radio. Watch for words that are used to convince consumers to buy catalog items. Keep a list of these "enticing" or "persuasive" or "deceptive" words. Make sure you understand how the words are being used to try to control or manipulate you.

- Choose 5 interesting words, or have someone choose them for you. Choose words that you do not know well. Write a dialogue or poem that uses the words.

- Choose an interesting word from the dictionary. Pick a word that is unfamiliar to you. Try to find one that has a sound you like. Now, get ready to SELL that word as the "world's best word," or the "world's most interesting word," or the "world's most important word." Make a poster, banner, or other kind of advertisement to promote that word.

- Choose a word, or have someone choose a word for you.
    Write rhyming words.
    Use it to make new words.
    List synonyms.
    List antonyms.
    List homonyms or homographs *(if there are any)*.
    Write a story, joke, or advertisement about the word.
    Look up the meaning in your dictionary.
    Draw it on paper so its shape shows the word's feeling or meaning.
    Write, draw, paint, or cut out the word repeatedly to make a collage.

- Keep a list of colorful or effective phrases that you find or write:
    phrases with pizzazz
    phrases that make you hear certain sounds
    phrases that arouse your curiosity
    phrases that make you feel something
    phrases that just grab your attention
    phrases that make you taste something
    phrases that build suspense

Writing Yellow Pages, Rev. Ed.

- Be on the lookout for a phrase that causes a picture to appear in your mind. Get some colored construction paper or poster paper. Tear shapes out of the paper to create the picture that is in your mind. Use only torn paper. Do not use scissors. Paste up the picture, and write the phrase across the bottom.

- Get an old picture frame. Remove the glass. Put a brightly-colored piece of paper inside the frame. Start collecting "Words to Show Off." These should be words that you love, for ANY reason. Fill your frame with your favorite words. Then replace the glass. Use these words in your writing.

- Throw a word party. Decorate with words. Use great words on the invitations. Write words on cookies and cakes. Use the party as a place to show off things you have written.

- Pick a great word that you think your classmates will NOT know. Write a question with that word in it. Ask your classmates to answer the question. In order to answer the question, each classmate will have to figure out what the word means!

- Read greeting cards to see what kinds of words are used for birthday, anniversary, Valentine, or other greetings. Design your own greeting cards complete with original messages from you.

- Collect words that start with one letter of the alphabet. Try writing sentences, short poems, or even whole paragraphs and stories that use many, many of the words.

- Use large mural paper to make cut-out tracings of yourself. Do this with a friend. Lie down on the mural paper while your friend traces the outline of your body. Cut out the shape. Use it as a spot for collecting great words that describe people. *(Collect words that describe appearance, actions, or personality.)*

- Hang a huge, blank mural on your wall. Use it to collect puns, idioms, great quotations, colorful phrases, important sayings, or any other interesting word combinations

- Read cookbooks, game books, and other books giving directions in a sequential manner. Make a list of the words used frequently to tell the reader "what to do," "when to do," and "how to do."

- Choose a career or profession. Find 50 words that could be used in connection with that job.

- Hold a word parade. Write great words on posters. Illustrate the words. Put the posters on sticks and parade through the school or neighborhood.

- Pick out interesting rhyming word combinations as you read poetry. Keep your own list of rhyming words.

- Find a short piece of writing *(yours or someone else's)*. Circle all the words that are rather ordinary. Try to replace each of those words with a different word that is more powerful, colorful, fresh, specific, or interesting.

WORDS TO COLLECT AND USE

Make lists of words. Keep the lists to help improve your writing. Start with these collections, then add other kinds of words that you think you might need.

artistic words	happy words	adventuresome words
city words	tough words	circus words
country words	slippery words	goodbye words
earth words	sloppy words	hello words
water words	brilliant words	travel words
short words	sound words	scratchy words
long words	funny words	yes words
little words	juicy words	no words
big words	scary words	size words
soft words	busy words	shape words
loud words	boasting words	weather words
slow words	soothing words	career words
fast words	movement words	teenage words
indoor words	nonsense words	teacher words
outdoor words	timid words	words with pizzazz
summer words	generous words	nature words
winter words	thirsty words	plant words
lazy words	touch words	frightening words
ambitious words	taste words	healthy words
animal words	smell words	complicated words
people words	tricky words	odd words
colorful words	smooth words	hungry words
cold words	windy words	lonely words
hot words	invented words	heavy words
day words	conceited words	cheerful words
night words	music words	dark words
wet words	fresh words	light words
dry words	math words	hospital words
sticky words	history words	prickly words
feeling words	science words	outrageous words
friendly words	geography words	mysterious words
sound words	travel words	love words
fashion words	space words	joking words
food words	complimenting words	warning words
family words	peacemaking words	underwater words
holiday words	troublemaking words	emergency words
jungle words	breathtaking words	exercise words
sad words	convincing words	spooky words
	suspense words	

Writing Yellow Pages, Rev. Ed.

DESCRIPTIVE WORDS

ADJECTIVES *(words that describe persons, places, or things)*

abominable
abrupt
absurd
aggressive
appreciative
archaic
atrocious
avid

beautiful
bibulous
bountiful
brackish
brilliant
brusque
bubbly

cankerous
cathartic
charismatic
charming
coarse
colorful
comely
compassionate
contentious

daft
dangerous
dauntless
decorative
delirious
dexterous
dour
dowdy
dreary
dubious

eager
effervescent
elaborate
electrifying
elegant

fabulous
fascinating
feeble
fervent
fetid
fluorescent
fulgent
futile

gaudy
generous
glib
glorious
gorgeous
gregarious
gushing

handsome
harmonious
haughty
hazardous
hilarious
horrendous
hysterical

illustrious
immaculate
impetuous
incredulous
ingenious
intriguing

jaunty
jocular
jolly
jubilant
judicious

kaleidoscopic
kind
knavish
knowledgeable
kooky

laborious
lank
lazy
leisurely
lethargic
logical
luminous
lush

magical
magnanimous
magnificent
majestic
massive
monstrous
mystical

natural
nauseous
negligent
nonchalant
notorious
nutty

obedient
obnoxious
obstinate
offensive
ordinary
outrageous

painful
palpable
peaceful
pensive
pleasant
putrid

quaint
quartz
queasy
quirky

radiant
raucous
remorseful
repugnant
respectful
ridiculous
rollicking
rude

satirical
scrawny
scrupulous
sharp
sluggish
spectacular
splendid
sweltering

taut
tempestuous
tenacious
terrific
torrid
tremulous
tyrannical

ultraviolet
uncommon
undulant
unique
unwieldy

valiant
venomous
verbose
vivacious
volatile
vulnerable

wacky
whimsical
wiggly
withdrawn
witty

ADVERBS *(words that describe actions)*

above
absolutely
abundantly
accidentally
afterward
already
almost
always
amazingly
angrily
anywhere
anxiously
audibly
away

badly
barely
beforehand
belatedly
below
best
better
brashly
brilliantly
briskly
brutally
busily

carefully
cleverly
completely
conditionally
consequently
considerably
consistently
constantly
conveniently
cordially
currently

deceitfully
decidedly
demurely
differently

earlier
early
easily
effectively
even
eventually
ever
everywhere
exactly
extremely

falsely
far
fast
farther
farthest
faster
fastest
fiercely
finally
flagrantly
foolishly
forcibly
forever
frankly
frequently
frivolously
further
furthermore
furthest

generously
gently
gradually
gratefully

hard
hardly
hastily
heartily
hopefully
hypothetically

immediately
importantly
independently
inside

joyfully
justly

lately
later
less
least
long

marginally
meaningfully
merrily
more
most
mostly

narrowly
near
neatly
never
noisily
not
notably
now
nowhere

occasionally
often
outside

partially
poorly
positively
precisely
presently
provisionally

quickly
quietly
quite

really
recently
relatively
remarkably

sadly
secondly
seldom
severely
sharply
short
significantly
simply
sometimes
somewhere
soon
soundly
surely
surprisingly

terribly
then
there
tightly
tomorrow

unconditionally
unexpectedly
uniquely
unusually
usually

weakly
well
wholly
worse
worst

WORDS THAT SHOW ACTION

abandon
abolish
acquit
agitate
argue
astound
attack

babble
balance
beat
beg
blubber
bubble
bother
bounce
break
brush
burst
bustle

capture
carry
catapult
catch
cavort
chase
chatter
cheer
choke
chew
climb
clobber
conquer
cough
crackle
cram
crash
creep
crumble
crumple

dance
dangle
dart

dash
demolish
destroy
devour
dive
drag
drool

eject
erase
escape
evaporate
explode
explore

fiddle
fidget
fight
fizzle
flash
flaunt
flee
flicker
float
flop
flounder
flutter
frolic

gag
gargle
gasp
giggle
gloat
gnash
gobble
gore
grasp
gush
guzzle

hobble
hurl
hurtle
hustle

incite
imitate
insist

jiggle
jostle
juggle
jump

kick
kiss

laugh
leap
lumber

mangle
measure
melt
mumble
mutter

pester
plummet
plunge
pump
puncture
push

quake
quibble
quiver

race
rescue
romp
rumble
rupture
rush

scamper
scatter
scramble
scream
scribble
scurry
seize
shake
shiver
shriek
shock
shuffle
simmer
sing
sink
sizzle
skid
skip
slice
slide
sling
slink
slither
slobber
smash
sneak
sniff
sob
split
spout
squeal
squeeze
snatch
sneer
sneeze
snort
snuggle
sparkle
spit
splatter
stab
stalk
steal
stomp

storm
strike
stroke
stroll
struggle
stumble
stutter
suspend
swallow
swarm
swat
swim
swirl

tackle
tattle
tease
throw
tickle
toss
trounce
trudge
tumble
twirl
twist
twitch
twitter

usurp

vanquish

wallow
whimper
whine
whip
whirl
wiggle
wink
wobble
wrestle
wriggle

BETTER WAYS WITH ORDINARY WORDS

Synonyms for Words Frequently Used in Students' Writing

afraid — fearful, alarmed, timid, apprehensive, frightened, terrified, anxious, insecure, cowardly, suspicious, mistrustful

amazing — incredible, unbelievable, improbable, fabulous, wonderful, fantastic, astonishing, astounding, extraordinary

angry — mad, furious, enraged, excited, wrathful, indignant, exasperated, aroused, inflamed

answer — reply, respond, retort, acknowledge

ask — question, inquire of, seek information from, put a question to, demand, request, expect, inquire, query, interrogate, examine, quiz

awful — dreadful, terrible, abominable, bad, poor, unpleasant

bad — evil, immoral, wicked, corrupt, sinful, depraved, rotten, contaminated, spoiled, tainted, harmful, injurious, unfavorable, defective, inferior, imperfect, substandard, faulty, improper, inappropriate, unsuitable, disagreeable, unpleasant, cross, nasty, unfriendly, irascible, horrible, atrocious, outrageous, scandalous, infamous, wrong, noxious, sinister, putrid, snide, deplorable, dismal, gross, heinous, nefarious, base, obnoxious, detestable, despicable, contemptible, foul, rank, ghastly, execrable

beautiful — pretty, lovely, handsome, attractive, gorgeous, dazzling, splendid, magnificent, comely, fair, ravishing, graceful, elegant, fine, exquisite, aesthetic, pleasing, shapely, delicate, stunning, glorious, heavenly, resplendent, radiant, glowing, blooming, sparkling

begin — start, open, launch, initiate, commence, inaugurate, originate

big — enormous, huge, immense, gigantic, vast, colossal, gargantuan, large, sizeable, grand, great, tall, substantial, mammoth, astronomical, ample, broad, expansive, spacious, stout, tremendous, titanic, mountainous

brave — courageous, fearless, dauntless, intrepid, plucky, daring, heroic, valorous, audacious, bold, gallant, valiant

break — fracture, rupture, shatter, smash, wreck, crash, demolish

bright — shining, shiny, gleaming, brilliant, sparkling, shimmering, radiant, vivid, colorful, lustrous, luminous, incandescent, intelligent, knowing, quick-witted, smart, intellectual

boring — dull, doleful, stolid, dismal, gloomy, dowdy, tiresome

Writing Yellow Pages, Rev. Ed.

calm — quiet, peaceful, still, tranquil, mild, serene, smooth, composed, collected, unruffled, level-headed, unexcited, detached, aloof

cool — chilly, cold, frosty, wintry, icy, frigid

crooked — bent, twisted, curved, hooked, zigzag

cry — shout, yell, yowl, scream, roar, bellow, weep, wail, sob, bawl

cut — gash, slash, nick, sever, slice, carve, cleave, slit, chop, crop, lop, reduce

dangerous — perilous, hazardous, risky, uncertain, unsafe

dark — shadowy, unlit, murky, gloomy, dim, dusky, shaded, sunless, black, dismal, sad

decide — determine, settle, choose, resolve

definite — certain, sure, positive, determined, clear, distinct, obvious

delicious — savory, delectable, appetizing, luscious, scrumptious, palatable, delightful, enjoyable, exquisite

describe — portray, characterize, picture, narrate, relate, recount, represent, report

destroy — ruin, demolish, raze, waste, kill, slay, end, extinguish

difference — disagreement, inequality, contrast, dissimilarity, incompatibility

dull — boring, tiring, tiresome, uninteresting, slow, dumb, stupid, unimaginative, lifeless, dead, insensible, tedious, wearisome, listless, expressionless, plain, monotonous, humdrum, dreary

eager — keen, fervent, enthusiastic, involved, interested, alive to

empty — uninhabited, void, destitute, vacant, vacuous, deserted

end — stop, finish, terminate, conclude, close, halt, cessation, discontinuance

enjoy — appreciate, delight in, to be pleased with, indulge in, luxuriate in, bask in, relish, savor, like

explain — elaborate, clarify, define, interpret, justify, account for

fair — just, impartial, unbiased, objective, unprejudiced, honest

fall — drop, descend, plunge, topple, tumble

false — fake, fraudulent, counterfeit, spurious, untrue, unfounded, erroneous, deceptive, groundless, fallacious

famous — well-known, renowned, celebrated, famed, eminent, illustrious, distinguished, noted, notorious

fast — quick, rapid, swift, speedy, fleet, hasty, snappy, mercurial, swiftly, rapidly, quickly, snappily, speedily, lickety-split, posthaste, hastily, expeditiously, like a flash

fat — stout, corpulent, fleshy, beefy, paunchy, plump, full, rotund, tubby, pudgy, cubby, chunky, bulky, elephantine, obese

fear — fright, dread, terror, alarm, dismay, anxiety, awe, horror, panic, apprehension

fly — soar, hover, flit, wing, flee, waft, glide, coast, skim, sail, cruise

funny — humorous, amusing, droll, comic, comical, laughable, silly

get — acquire, obtain, secure, procure, gain, fetch, find, accumulate, win, earn, reap, catch, net, bag, derive, collect, gather, gleam, pick up, accept, come by, regain, salvage

go — recede, depart, fade, disappear, move, travel, proceed

good — excellent, fine, superior, wonderful, marvelous, suited, suitable, proper, capable, generous, kindly, friendly, gracious, obliging, pleasant, agreeable, pleasurable, satisfactory, well-behaved, obedient, honorable, reliable, trustworthy, favorable, profitable, advantageous, righteous, expedient, helpful, valid, genuine, ample, salubrious, estimable, beneficial, splendid, great, noble, worthy, first-rate, top-notch, grand, superb, respectable

great — noteworthy, worthy, distinguished, remarkable, grand, considerable, powerful, much, mighty

gross — improper, rude, coarse, indecent, crude, vulgar, outrageous, extreme, grievous, shameful, uncouth, obscene, low

happy — pleased, contented, satisfied, delighted, elated, joyful, cheerful, ecstatic, jubilant, gay, tickled, gratified, glad, blissful, overjoyed

hate — despise, loathe, detest, abhor, disfavor, dislike, disapprove, abominate

have — hold, possess, own, contain, acquire, gain, maintain, bear, beget, occupy, absorb, fill

help — aid, assist, support, encourage, back, wait on, attend, serve, relieve, succor, benefit, befriend, abet

hide — conceal, cover, mask, cloak, camouflage, screen, shroud, veil

hurry — rush, run, speed, race, hasten, accelerate, bustle

important — necessary, vital, critical, indispensable, valuable, essential, significant, primary, principal, considerable, famous, distinguished, notable, well-known

interesting — fascinating, engaging, sharp, keen, bright, intelligent, animated, spirited, attractive, inviting, intriguing, provocative, thought-provoking, challenging, inspiring, involving, moving, titillating, tantalizing, exciting, entertaining, piquant, lively, racy, spicy, engrossing, absorbing, consuming, gripping, arresting, enthralling, spellbinding, curious, captivating, enchanting, bewitching, appealing

keep — hold, retain, withhold, preserve, maintain, sustain, support

lazy — indolent, slothful, idle, inactive, sluggish

like — adore, admire, glorify, praise, worship, idolize, venerate

little — tiny, small, diminutive, shrimp, runt, miniature, puny, exiguous, dinky, cramped, limited, itty-bitty, microscopic, slight, petite, minute

look — gaze, see, glance, watch, survey, study, seek, search for, peek, peep, glimpse, stare, contemplate, examine, gape, ogle, scrutinize, inspect, leer, behold, observe, view, witness, perceive, spy, sight, discover, notice, recognize, peer, eye, gawk, peruse, explore

love — admire, esteem, fancy, care for, cherish, adore, treasure, worship, appreciate, savor

make — create, originate, invent, beget, form, construct, design, fabricate, manufacture, produce, build, develop, do, effect, execute, compose, perform, accomplish, earn, gain, obtain, acquire, get

mark — label, tag, price, ticket, impress, trace, imprint, stamp, brand, sign, note, heed, notice, designate

mean — cruel, hard-hearted, inhuman, savage, barbarous, pitiless, ruthless, brutal, harsh, despicable, dishonorable, low, vulgar, vile

mischievous — prankish, playful, naughty, roguish, waggish, impish, sportive

moody — temperamental, changeable, short-tempered, glum, morose, sullen, irritable, testy, peevish, fretful, spiteful, sulky, touchy

move — plod, go, creep, crawl, inch, poke, drag, toddle, shuffle, trot, dawdle, walk, traipse, mosey, jog, plug, trudge, lumber, lag, run, sprint, trip, bound, hotfoot, high-tail, streak, stride, tear, breeze, whisk, rush, dash, dart, bolt, scamper, scurry, skedaddle, scoot, scuttle, scramble, race, chase, hasten, hurry, gallop, lope, accelerate, stir, budge, travel, wander, roam, journey, trek, ride, slip, glide, slide, slither, coast, sail, saunter, hobble, amble, stagger, prance, straggle, meander, perambulate, waddle, wobble, promenade, lunge

mysterious — hidden, secretive, puzzling, unexplained, inexplicable, obscure, dim

neat — clean, orderly, tidy, trim, dapper, smart, elegant, organized, spruced up, shipshape, well-kept

new — fresh, unique, original, unusual, modern, current, recent

nice — smooth, delicate, grand, refined, excellent, superior, showy, elegant, graceful, fair, comely, adorable, lovely, charming, delightful, dainty, neat, agreeable, pleasant, fastidious

old — feeble, frail, ancient, aged, used, worn, dilapidated, ragged, faded, broken-down, former, old-fashioned, outmoded, passe, veteran, mature, venerable, primitive, traditional, archaic, conventional, customary, stale, musty, obsolete

part — portion, share, piece, allotment, section, fraction, fragment

place — space, area, spot, region, location, position, residence, swelling, set, site, station, status, state

plan — plot, scheme, design, draw, map, diagram, procedure, arrangement, intention, contrivance, method, way, blueprint

popular — well-liked, approved, accepted, favorite, celebrated, common, current

proud — arrogant, snobbish, conceited, haughty, vain, self-satisfied, boastful

put — place, set, attach, establish, assign, keep, save, set aside, effect, achieve, do, build

quiet — silent, still, soundless, mute, tranquil, peaceful, calm, restful

right — correct, accurate, factual, true, good, just, honest, upright, lawful, moral, proper, suitable, apt, legal, fair

run — race, speed, hurry, hasten, sprint, dash, rush, escape, elope, flee

sad — miserable, forlorn, pitiable, disconsolate, serious, grave, gloomy, downcast, sorrowful, mournful, distressed, dejected, cheerless

say/tell — inform, notify, advise, relate, recount, narrate, explain, reveal, disclose, divulge, declare, command, order, bid enlighten, instruct, insist, teach, train, direct, issue, remark, converse, speak, affirm, utter, express, verbalize, voice, articulate, pronounce, deliver, convey, impart, assert, state, allege, mutter, mumble, whisper, sigh, exclaim, yell, sing, yelp, snarl, hiss, grunt, snort, roar, bellow, thunder, boom, scream, shriek, screech, squawk, whine, philosophize, stammer, stutter, lisp, drawl, jabber, announce, swear, vow

scared — afraid, frightened, alarmed, terrified, panicked, fearful, unnerved, insecure, timid, shy, skittish, jumpy, disquieted, worried, vexed, troubled, disturbed, horrified, terrorized, shocked, petrified, timorous, shrinking, tremulous, stupefied, paralyzed, stunned, apprehensive

scary — mysterious, secret, murky, shadowy, creepy, secret, dismal, grim, frightful, horrendous, dreaded, terrible, horrid

show — unhurried, gradual, leisurely, late, behind, tedious, slack

silly — brainless, ridiculous, nonsensical, absurd, foolish, crazed, idiotic, preposterous

smart — able, clever, talented, quick, expert, quick-witted, skillful, gifted, sharp, bright

stop — cease, halt, pause, discontinue, conclude, end, finish, quit

story — tale, myth, legend, fable, yarn, account, narrative, chronicle, epic, anecdote, memoir

strange — odd, peculiar, unusual, unfamiliar, uncommon, queer, weird, outlandish, curious, unique, exclusive, irregular

surprise — alarm, scare, appal, shock, frighten, affright, astound, dismay, daunt

take — hold, catch, seize, grasp, win, capture, acquire, pick, choose, select, remove, steal, lift, rob, engage, purchase, buy, retract, recall, occupy, consume

tell — disclose, reveal, show, expose, uncover, relate, narrate, inform, advise, explain, divulge, declare, command, order, bid, recount, repeat

think — judge, deem, assure, believe, consider, contemplate, reflect, meditate

trick — deceive, beguile, delude, dupe, mislead, ensnare, entrap, betray

trouble — distress, anguish, anxiety, worry, wretchedness, pain, danger, peril, disaster, grief, misfortune, difficulty, concern, inconvenience, effort

true — accurate, right, proper, precise, exact, valid, genuine, real, actual, steady, loyal, dependable, sincere

ugly — hideous, frightful, frightening, shocking, horrible, unpleasant, monstrous, repulsive, terrifying, gross, gruesome, grisly, ghastly, horrid, unsightly, plain, homely, unattractive

unhappy — miserable, uncomfortable, wretched, heartbroken, unfortunate, downhearted, sorrowful, depressed, dejected, melancholy, glum, gloomy, dismal, discouraged, sad

wonderful — extraordinary, uncommon, peculiar, marvelous, remarkable, preposterous, amazing, wondrous, striking miraculous, marvelous, astonishing, startling, superb

wrong — incorrect, inaccurate, mistaken, erroneous, improper, unsuitable

CONFUSING WORDS

ability (power)
capacity (condition)

accede (agree)
exceed (surpass)

accept (receive)
except (exclude)

adapt (adjust)
adopt (accept)

all ready (completely prepared)
already (previously)

allude (to refer to)
elude (escape)

allusion (reference)
illusion (false perception)
delusion (false belief)

assure (to set a person's mind at ease)
insure (guarantee life or property against harm)
ensure (to secure from harm)

avenge (to achieve justice)
revenge (retaliation)

averse (opposition on the subject's part)
adverse (opposition against the subject's will)

avoid (shun)
avert (turn away)

between (use when referring to two persons, places, or things)
among (use when referring to more than two persons, places, or things)

clench (to grip something tightly, as hand or teeth)
clinch (to fasten firmly together)

complement (something that completes)
compliment (an expression of praise)

confidant (one to whom secrets are told)
confidante (a female confidant)
confident (assured of success)

credible (plausible)
creditable (deserving commendation)
credulous (gullible)

deny (contradict)
refute (to give evidence to disprove something)

element (a basic assumption)
factor (something that contributes to a result)

elicit (to call forth)
illicit (unlawful)

eminent (prominent)
imminent (soon to occur)

fatal (causing death)
fateful (affecting one's destiny)

graceful (refers to movement)
gracious (courteous)

impassable (impossible to traverse)
impassive (devoid of emotion)

imply (to hint or suggest)
infer (to draw conclusions based on facts)

incredible (unbelievable)
incredulous (skeptical)

insignificant (trivial)
tiny (small)

insinuate (to hint covertly)
intimate (to imply subtly)

invoke (to call upon a higher power for assistance)
evoke (to elicit)

judicial (pertaining to law)
judicious (exhibiting sound judgment)

latter (the second of two things mentioned)
later (subsequently)

Writing Yellow Pages, Rev. Ed.

likely (use when mere probability is involved)
apt (use when a known tendency is involved)

mania (craze)
phobia (fear)

nauseated (to feel queasy)
nauseous (causing queasiness)

oblige (to feel a debt of gratitude)
obligate (under direct compulsion to follow a certain course)

official (authorized by a proper authority)
officious (extremely eager to offer help or advice)

older (refers to persons and things)
elder (refers to only one person)

oral (refers to the sense of "word of mouth;" cannot refer to written words)
verbal (can refer to both written and spoken words)

partly (use when stress is placed on a part in contrast to the whole)
partially (use when the whole is stressed, often indirectly)

persecute (to oppress or harass)
prosecute (to initiate legal or criminal action against)

piteous (pathetic)
pitiable (lamentable)
pitiful (very inferior or insignificant)

practically (almost)
virtually (to all intents)

precipitant (rash, impulsive)
precipitate (to hurl downward)
precipitous (extremely steep)

principal (chief)
principle (basic law or truth)

raise (to move upward; to build; to breed)
rear (to bring up a child)
rise (to ascend)

rare (refers to unusual value and quality of which there is a permanent small supply)
scarce (refers to temporary infrequency)

ravage (to devastate or despoil)
ravish (to take away by force)

recourse (an application to something for aid or support)
resource (an available supply)

regretful (sorrowful)
regrettable (something that elicits mental distress)

reluctant (unwilling)
reticent (refers to a temperament or style that is characteristically silent or restrained)

repel (drive off; cause distaste or aversion)
repulse (drive off; reject by means of discourtesy)

respectfully (showing honor and esteem)
respectively (one at a time in order)

restive (resistance to control)
restless (lacking repose)

specific (explicitly set forth)
particular (not general or universal)

stationary (immovable)
stationery (matched writing paper and envelopes)

tasteful (exhibiting that which is proper or seemly in a social setting)
tasty (having a pleasing flavor)

transient (refers to what literally stays for only a short time)
transitory (short-lived, impermanent)

turbid (muddy, dense; in turmoil)
turgid (swollen, grandiloquent)

RHYMING WORDS

Great for writing poetry!

dish
fish
squish
swish
wish

bat
begat
cat
fat
flat
hat
mat
pat
rat
sat
slat
splat
that

and
band
brand
canned
fanned
gland
grand
hand
land
sand
stand

day
delay
clay
gay
gray
hay
lay
may
play
ray
say
stray
tray
way

cream
dream
gleam
scream
seam
steam
team

bunk
chunk
clunk
drunk

hunk
junk
plunk
punk
skunk
stunk
sunk
trunk

air
bare
bear
care
bear
bare
dare
ere
fair
fare
flare
hair
heir
hare
mare
pair
pare
pear
rare
stair
stare
there
wear
where

career
cheer
clear
ear
dear
deer
fear
hear
here
jeer
mere
near
peer
queer
rear
sheer
steer
year

ahoy
boy
coy
enjoy
joy
toy

all
ball
call
crawl
fall
gall
hall
mall
stall
tall
wall

curl
furl
girl
hurl
pearl
swirl
twirl

back
black
clack
crack
hack
jack
lack
pack
quack
rack
sack
smack
stack
tack
track

by
bye
cry
eye
fry
high
I
lie
my
pie
shy
sigh
sty
tie
why
wry

beak
cheek
creak
creek
geek
leak
meek
peak
peek
reek
seek
sneak
weak
week

Writing Yellow Pages, Rev. Ed.

block
clock
cock
dock
flock
frock
knock
lock
mock
rock
shock
sock
tock

core
door
floor
four
more
pour
roar
sore
store
tore
wore

attach
batch
catch
hatch
latch
match
patch

blink
brink
clink
drink
link
pink
rink
sink
shrink
stink
think
wink

blue
clue
crew
dew
do
drew
few
flew
glue
grew
knew
new
to
too
two
true

bend
blend
end
friend
lend
mend
pretend
rend
send
spend
tend

above
dove
glove
love
of
shove

rain
cane
gain
lain
main
pain
plane
stain
train
vain

ate
bait
date
fate
gate
grate
great
hate
late
mate
rate
state
wait

bold
bowled
cold
fold
gold
hold
mold
old
polled
rolled
sold
told

bliss
hiss
kiss
miss
sis
this

cog
dog
fog
flog
frog
hog
jog
log
smog

aid
aide
blade
fade
glade
grade
laid
made
maid
paid
raid
stayed
strayed
wade

bloom
broom
doom
gloom
groom
loom
room
tomb
zoom

burn
churn
earn
fern
learn
stern
turn
urn
yearn

bought
brought
caught
fought
ought
sought
taught
taut
thought

bean
clean
dean
gene
glean
green
keen
lean
mean
preen
queen
scene
seen
teen

bun
done
fun
gun
none
one
pun
run
sun
ton
won

chime
crime
dime
grime
lime
mime
rhyme
slime
time

book
brook
cook
crook
hook
look
rook
shook
took

ajar	**bite**	**bowl**	**fix**	**blow**
are	bright	coal	kicks	crow
bar	fight	foal	licks	floe
car	invite	hole	mix	flow
far	kite	mole	nix	go
jar	knight	pole	picks	know
mar	light	roll	six	low
tar	lite	sole	sticks	mow
scar	mite	soul	ticks	no
star	night		wicks	oh
	quite	**dine**		owe
cap	right	fine	**ban**	row
chap	rite	line	can	sew
clap	sight	mine	fan	show
flap	site	nine	man	snow
gap	slight	pine	pan	so
knap	spike	shine	plan	stow
lap	tight	sign	ran	toe
map	white	swine	tan	tow
nap		tine	van	
slap	**be**	vine		**ail**
strap	bee	whine	**bing**	bail
tap	flea		bring	bale
trap	flee	**bone**	cling	dale
wrap	free	clone	ding	fail
	glee	cone	fling	flail
fist	he	groan	king	frail
grist	key	grown	ping	gale
hissed	knee	hone	ring	hail
insist	lee	known	sing	hale
kissed	me	lone	sling	jail
list	sea	moan	sting	mail
mist	see	own	swing	male
twist	tea	phone	wing	nail
	tee	sown		pail
bin	three	stone	**been**	pale
chin	tree	thrown	den	quail
din	we	tone	hen	rail
fin		zone	men	sale
gin	**chive**		pen	shale
in	dive		ten	tail
kin	drive		when	tale
pin	five		yen	trail
sin	hive			wail
skin	I've			whale
tin	jive			
win	live			

Writing Yellow Pages, Rev. Ed.

THE WRITING PROCESS

STEP 1 ROMANCING

. . . a group experience, an individual experience, a thought, a piece of literature, an unexpected happening, a common feeling, a question, a memory, a discussion, a shocking happening, a surprise event, an activity in a content area—anything that sparks writing!

This is the reason for writing . . . the motivator . . . the spark that gets ideas brewing. It may start with an activity designed by a teacher, or writers may grab onto something that's already there inside them. Spend plenty of time on this step. When writers can't think of anything to say, or do not want to write, it is usually because they have not been sufficiently romanced!

STEP 2 COLLECTING

. . . the gathering of ideas, words, fragments, thoughts, facts, phrases, questions, and observations

This is the most fun and creative part of the writing process. It is the stage where writers brainstorm, sometimes alone, and sometimes with others. It's the time to gather all the bits and pieces of words and ideas that will become the piece of writing. Take plenty of time for collecting. Write down everything. A writer can always eliminate, expand, and combine ideas later.

STEP 3 ORGANIZING

. . . the time for taking a close look at all those words, phrases, and ideas you have collected and think about what fits with what

In this step, writer's look closely at what has been collected, and begin to pull ideas together in some way. This might be done with lines and arrows, diagrams, clusters, outlines, webs, or lists. During the organizing step, a writer might find some facts or ideas missing. She might go back for a bit to step two to gather some more good stuff to fit into the organizational plan!

STEP 4 DRAFTING

. . . the pull-it-together stage

Here is where the writing of whole lines and sentences actually begins. The writer looks at the groupings or outline and starts to put ideas, words, and phrases together into lines, sentences, and paragraphs. Take time for this step. Remember that it is a ROUGH draft. It does not have to be final or complete. There is time for adding, changing, subtracting, and rearranging later.

STEP 5 REVIEWING

. . . the author's chance to get the draft out in the open and see how it looks or hear how it sounds

At this point, the writer gives a quick overview to the piece, perhaps reading it aloud. This allows the writer to think about whether it makes sense or sounds right, and if, in general, it says what was intended.

STEP 6 SHARING FOR PRAISE & QUESTIONS

. . . a time for trading pieces, reading in a small group, or sharing with the teacher or another writer—for the purpose of getting a response to the writing

The writer asks someone else to review and respond to the writing. That response can be in the form of praise or compliments (pointing out strengths). Or, it can be in the form of questions that get the writer thinking about how to make the writing more clear, interesting, or effective. In both cases, the response needs to be specific, helpful, supportive, and non-attacking to the writer.

Sample praise: Your phrase *icy fingers of fog* really made me feel that fog!
Your opening word, *Crash!,* really grabbed my attention. Great beginning!

Sample questions: Did you mean to give the ending away so soon?
I didn't hear how the girls got into the volcano. Could you make that more clear?

STEP 7 EDITING/REVISING

. . . the changing & fixing step . . . including anything from reshuffling or replacing words to reworking whole pieces

Making use of the response gained from other readers (as well as her/his own thoughts and discoveries about the writing), the writer revises, replaces, adds, deleted, rearranges, or otherwise strengthens and changes the pieces.

STEP 8 CHECKING MECHANICS

. . . a time to inspect the writing closely for the mechanical mistakes

This is the time for checking and correcting spelling, punctuation, capitalization, sentence structure, and grammatical construction. Some of that may happen automatically in other steps, but this is the time to focus on it. The writer may need assistance from a peer, teacher, editing committee, or adult helper for this step.

STEP 9 FINAL POLISHING

. . . the writing of the final draft—making use of your own ideas for improvement and the suggestions of others

In this step, the writer has decided that he or she knows what is needed to move toward a final, accurate copy. Taking the advice of others, and making the best use he or she can of the results of stages 6, 7, and 8, the writer prepares a polished piece. This copy may be "polished" or finalized in many forms (hand written, typed on computer, dictated to an older helper, recorded on tape, etc.).

STEP 10 SHOWING OFF

. . . the sharing, publishing, or showing-off part—the chance to use your written words to communicate with others

The writer should always have the option of sharing, publishing, or otherwise showcasing the writing. If the author chooses to make the piece public, there are unlimited ways to do this. Writers should be encouraged to find inviting and non-threatening ways to share their writing.

LITERARY DEVICES

alliteration .... *repeated consonant sounds in a phrase or sentence*

Alliteration usually appears at the beginning of words. It sets a rhythm or mood to sentences or phrases. It is fun and pleasing to the ear.

Ex: Seven slippery snakes slithered silently south.

---

characterization .... *techniques a writer uses to let the reader know about the characters*

This allows readers to know about a character's personality, appearance, motivations, or behaviors.

---

figurative language ... *a way of using language that expands the literal meaning of the words and gives them a new or more interesting twist*

Metaphors, similes, puns, and idioms are examples of figurative language.

---

foreshadowing .... *subtle suggestions within the text or story that give the reader hints about something that may happen later in the story*

This technique increases suspense and leads the reader to anticipate events to come.

---

hyperbole .... *extreme exaggeration used to increase the effect of a statement*

This serves to add humor and imagination to particular types of writing, such as tall tales. It also adds emphasis to a point a speaker or a writer is trying to make.

Ex: I've asked you a million times to clean your room.

---

imagery .... *details that appeal to the senses*

Imagery makes the experience more real!

Ex: Sweet, slow drops of deep purple juice drip from the corners of my mouth and flow in little blueberry rivers down to my chin.

---

irony .... *a discrepancy between what is said and what is meant, or between what appears to be true and what is really true*

It is ironic when a mother, discovering her child has scribbled on the walls of her living room with permanent marker says, "Now, isn't this lovely!" It is also ironic in a story when a happy-go-lucky, friendly clown turns out to be the saddest person in the world.

metaphor .... *a comparison between two things that are not ordinarily alike*

Like other figurative language, metaphors make writing fresh, moving, interesting, humorous, or touching.

Ex: My little brother is like a tornado.
    Life is a gift, waiting to be opened.
    Without you, I'm a leaf tossed in a cyclone.
    The toaster attacks my toast with its tongue of fire.

---

mood .... *the feeling in a piece of writing*

Mood is set by a combination of the words and sounds used, the setting, the imagery, and the details. Mood may give a feeling of mystery, rush, softness, cold, fear, darkness, etc.

---

onomatopoeia .... *use of a word that makes the same sound as its meaning, or a word that sounds like the same sound that an object actually makes*

The use of onomatopoeia adds auditory appeal, and makes the writing more interesting.

Ex: The fire crackles and spits, pops, and hisses.

---

parody .... *a work that makes fun of another work by imitating some aspect of the other writer's style*

A parody is often enjoyable to readers because it humorously exaggerates features of the work it is imitating, in order to convey a message, launch a critique, or just amuse the reader.

---

personification .... *giving human characteristics to a nonliving object*

Personification compares two dissimilar things by attributing human thoughts, feelings, appearances, actions, or attitudes to an object or animal.

Ex: The lightning reached down with forked fingers and scratched the ground.
    A massive rock bridge gazes up at the cloudless sky
    Whipping wind licks at my chapped face.
    The river sings a lazy, bubbling tune to me

---

plot .... *a series of events that the writer uses to make a story*

The plot usually contains the telling of a situation or problem, the development of the situation to a peak of action (the climax), and a final resolving of the problem or situation.

Writing Yellow Pages, Rev. Ed.

point of view	***lets the reader know who is telling the story***
	The story may be told by a character in the story, a narrator who is in the story, or a narrator who is not in the story. Within the story, a character may tell the story about himself or herself (first person), or about others (with or without including herself or himself). Some stories have a series of narrators, speaking in first or second person.
rhyme	***repeating of sounds***
	Rhymes may occur at the ends of lines, or within the lines.
	Ex: There once was a gal from Dubuque ***who was anxious to marry a duke.*** ***Ex: The kite was sliding and gliding, slipping and flipping.***
satire	***writing that makes fun of the shortcomings of people, systems, or institutions for the purpose of enlightening readers and/or bringing about a change***
	Satires are often written about governmental systems of persons of power and influence. They can range from light fun-making to harsh, bitter mockery.
setting	***the place where a story or event occurs***
	The setting may be real or imaginary. Setting also includes the time period covered by the story.
simile	***a comparison between two unlike things, using the word like or as to connect the two***
	Like other figures of speech, similes make writing fresh, interesting, moving, humorous, or touching. They surprise and delight the reader, and make the description or explanation more real to the reader.
	Ex: July moves as slowly as a sleepy snail. ***Life is like a dark pool of water.*** ***Math problems are like hot, boring days that never end.*** ***That idea is as empty as my bank account.***
theme	***the main meaning or idea of a piece of writing***
	It includes the topic and a viewpoint or opinion about the topic.
tone	***the approach a writer takes toward a topic***
	The tone may be playful, hostile, humorous, serious, argumentative, etc.

WRITING IDEAS:
WHAT WOULD YOU DO IF . . .

Write a complete paragraph, poem, letter, or essay answering one of the following questions:

What would you do if . . .

   . . . a tidal wave was headed for your home, town, or city?

   . . . you suspected your next door neighbor was a spy?

   . . . you overheard a damaging secret about a friend?

   . . . you mysteriously knew tomorrow's news today?

   . . . you had the power to change one thing about the world?

   . . . your home or school lost electrical power for a month?

   . . . no music was allowed to be made, sold, or played in the world?

   . . . you were being chased by an elephant from one direction and a rhino from another?

   . . . you received a threatening letter from a stranger?

   . . . you found yourself in a haunted house at midnight?

   . . . the principal asked you to take charge of the entire school for a day?

   . . . the only food you had to eat for a week was asparagus?

   . . . you met a fire-breathing dragon face to face?

   . . . someone left a baby in a basket on your doorstep?

   . . . you were accused of a crime you did not commit?

   . . . you found a wallet on the sidewalk containing five dollars?

   . . . you found a wallet on the sidewalk containing five hundred dollars?

   . . . a genie squeezed out of your orange juice carton to grant one wish for you?

   . . . your best friend was quarantined with a with a contagious disease for a month?

   . . . you broke out in a rash from head to toe on the doctor's day off?

   . . . you had to cross a river without a bridge or a boat?

   . . . you met a real leprechaun at midnight on St. Patrick's Day?

   . . . it rained continuously for forty days and forty nights?

   . . . while fishing in a pond near your home, you hooked an alligator?

   . . . someone delivered a hundred bushels of sweet corn [on the cob] to your home?

   . . . you awakened at your school desk and were told that you had been asleep for six weeks?

Writing Yellow Pages, Rev. Ed.

HOW TO . . .

Create a piece of writing that explains how to do one of these things. Make sure you write very clear instructions that a reader could follow. Even if the task is impossible or fanciful, the directions should be clear!

HOW TO . . .

clean up a mess . . . quickly	eat pizza
get on and off a ski lift	make a banana split
build a friendship	make friends with a panther
build the world's most awesome fort	replace a flat tire
build a go-cart	study for a test
drive a scooter	avoid a cold
make a mess	snowboard
stop a nosebleed	keep your mother happy
make a cheese souffle	cook perfect spaghetti
choose a friend	get rid of a sore throat
eat watermelon	save money
get out of bed in the morning	cure a headache
choose the perfect pair of jeans	iron a shirt
get out of trouble	make the perfect sandwich
ruin a friendship	avoid an argument
clean your room in five minutes	kick the TV habit
make a birdhouse	stop someone from snoring
lock a car	gain weight
choose a boyfriend (girlfriend)	deal with a bully
sky dive	write a rap song
climb a frozen waterfall	kill a wasp
SCUBA-dive	ask a girl (boy) on a date
make a milkshake	build your muscles
stay safe in a city	behave at a fancy dinner

THE TOP TEN

Write a list of ten things for one (or more) of these. The list can be 10 sentences, 10 phrases, 10 titles, 10 names, 10 labels, 10 words, or whatever other form fits the topic.

For each case, think of 10 ORIGINAL things. Avoid the ordinary items that everyone else might create.

THEN WRITE 10 . . .

- secrets that should be kept
- things to save
- substitutes for shoes
- smashing first lines for a mystery story
- titles for country songs
- ways to report on a book
- ways to serve potatoes
- things never to do again
- uses for ice cubes
- gifts to make for special occasions
- ideas for kinds of parties
- names for a pet fish
- ways to say "I love you."
- ways to say "I'm sorry."
- things to do before breakfast
- recipes using chocolate
- things that should be changed
- ideas for short stories
- uses for last year's calendar
- ways to help someone less fortunate
- games to play with three other people
- four-line rhymes
- outrageous words and their definitions
- holidays
- new subjects to study in school
- ways to honor senior citizens
- educational toys
- new colors

- new ice cream flavors
- themes for amusement parks
- names for roller coasters
- Halloween costumes
- uses for peach pits
- ways to paint a picture
- unique pizza toppings
- fetching first lines for limericks
- things to look for in a boyfriend
- things to look for in a girlfriend
- things to avoid in a boyfriend
- things to avoid in a girlfriend
- titles for patriotic songs
- uses for marshmallows
- places not to go on a vacation
- uses for kitty litter
- kinds of people to avoid
- suspenseful ending lines for a story
- ways to conserve natural resources
- reasons to clean your room
- never-before-tried sports
- things to say to a gorilla
- things not to say to a gorilla
- uses for paper clips
- names for a rock band
- titles for a joke book
- promises to keep
- things to watch out for

WRITING IDEAS:
STORY STARTERS

Never go to sleep with bubblegum in your mouth . . .

I should have known this was a terrible idea . . .

Miles and miles of scorching sand stretched ahead . . .

A huge, hairy, black creature lumbered toward the highway . . .

It was not until the boat had left the dock that he noticed . . .

Out of the darkness and into the campfire's light came . . .

Senators should be careful about what they eat . . .

Please don't say . . .

Suddenly, the sky lit up . . .

A piercing scream broke the stillness . . .

I was probably imagining this, but . . .

The crocodile opened its wide jaws, and . . .

I don't believe in magic pencils, but . . .

In a split second . . .

The fog set in at midday . . .

Where the tornado hit . . .

I'm sorry to tell you this, but . . .

As flood waters continued to rise . . .

Right in my own backyard . . .

Under the giant mushroom . . .

The day the teacher overslept, we . . .

The stone simply would not budge . . .

The driver looked away, just for a second, and . . .

A strange smell came from the swamp . . .

All the kids on the block waited anxiously as . . .

I became more frightened with every step . . .

My sister didn't believe I had seen the ghost until . . .

"Would I take you there if it were dangerous?" asked the . . .

The falls roared ahead of us in the dark as we paddled furiously . . .

Little did we know what was waiting around the corner . . .

A dark cloud covered the horizon, but it was not an ordinary cloud . . .

"Whatever made you think this would work?" asked the . . .

The curtains behind the dusty window parted slowly, and . . .

I've been chasing tornados for a long time, but this one . . .

When the power went out in the whole city, we were on . . .

We were awakened by the sound of glass breaking . . .

If you'll just give me a minute, I can convince you that . . .

"Trust me," she said, "you will really love this . . .

If I could tell those politicians a thing or two . . .

Oh, I wish I had never heard of the town of . . .

Never before have I been so humiliated . . .

This whole thing could have been avoided if . . .

Gigantic footprints led right up to the . . .

Under the pillow was a note which read . . . .

The whole town was in an uproar . . .

I felt my body shrinking, shrinking . . .

Okay, so horses aren't supposed to talk, but . . .

He stuck his hand into the opening and pulled out a . . .

It was just about time for the bell to ring at the end of the day when . . .

"Please get me out of here," came a weak voice from the . . .

Should I start with the part where the train disappeared or the part where . . .

You're probably wondering how three nice kids like us got into a . . .

If I live to be one hundred, I'll never forget . . .

"Open at your own risk" was written on the label of . . .

Another bar on the cage gave way and the lion . . .

The flashlight shined directly into my tent . . .

The ground began to sink down, down, down . . .

He's been missing for more than two days, and . . .

Suddenly the lantern sputtered and went out as . . .

A bent pocketknife is the only clue to . . .

More than anything in the world, she wanted . . .

The box opened slowly, and out came . . .

The fortuneteller was wrong about . . .

MIXING WRITING WITH CONTENT AREAS

Science

Prepare a **consumer's guide** of 50 ways to conserve water or power.

Create a friendly **user's guide** to the Internet.

Create a **science calendar**. Write and illustrate interesting scientific facts and discoveries on each month's page.

Compile a **handbook** of first aid procedures for a school, a home, or a camping trip.

Write an **ode** to an echinoderm, coelenterate, or mollusk.

Make a **recipe and menu book** containing menus for interesting, well-balanced meals.

Write the **biography** of a jellyfish or a tadpole.

Write some **lyrics** for a song to be sung by a stone-age "rock" group, Include names of some rocks and minerals in the song.

Make a **directory** of common diseases. Write a description of each disease and treatments for them.

Write a **resumé** of your qualifications to be class zoo-keeper or plant-tender.

Write a **tribute** to your teeth, hair, vocal chords, or muscles.

Write **directions** for making a bug-catcher or for preserving animal tracks.

Write a **tongue twister** about tongues or tendons.

After growing crystals, create crystal-shaped **poems**.

When you are studying the universe, write **space fantasies**.

Write **superstitions**. Explain scientifically why each superstition cannot be.

Write an **index** or a **table of contents** for a book on earthquakes, engines, or electricity.

Write a **myth** to explain weather conditions or any other phenomenon that persons long ago might not have understood.

Write **weather poems** or **personification stories** about clouds, hailstones, or tornadoes.

Write a **family album** about your own roots. Describe the traits you inherited.

Write **questions** for interviewing a geologist, microbiologist, chemist, hematologist, meteorologist, pharmacist, ichthyologist, or physicist.

Make a **directory** of plants, land forms, birds, arachnids, or reptiles. Draw 15 or more of each. Label and write distinguishing characteristics.

Adapted From IF YOU'RE TRYING TO TEACH KIDS HOW TO WRITE, YOU'VE GOT TO HAVE THIS BOOK!
©1995 by Incentive Publications, Inc. Nashville, TN. Used by permission.

Math

- Write an **essay** entitled "Ten Things You Should Know About Statistics."

- Write a **limerick** about an equation or an octagon.

- Write a **mystery story** titled, "The Case of the Missing Decimal Point."

- Write the **script** for a videotape explaining the basics of probability.

- Write a **dialogue** that would take place between the digits in the number 3,000,007.

- Write a **news article** about a kid who used math to solve a crime.

- Write a **joke** about long division, place value, or estimation.

- Make up **rhymes** that will help kids remember their multiplication facts.

- Write a **speech** that will convince someone to like math.

- Write a **love story** about a romance between a circle and a trapezoid.

- Write a **poem** using at least ten math words.

- Write a **play** about "The Wonderful World of Zero."

- Write **directions** for an original math game that will help players learn math facts.

- Write the **autobiography** of a right angle.

- Write a **diet** for an overweight ton.

- Write a **contract** between yourself and someone who is buying your bike on time payments.

- Write a **menu** for a restaurant where a family of four could dine for under $20.00.

- Make a "no number" **booklet** telling what the world would be like without numbers.

- Write a **song** that explains the operation of division.

- Compile your own math **dictionary** that has clear definitions of the math terms you use.

- Write an **ode** to the number 17 (or any other) telling why that number is special.

- Make **signs**, **posters**, and **advertising billboards** telling about the discounts that will be available at an upcoming sale.

- Make a **directory** of metric measures. Explain the metric system so that your directory could be used by someone who hasn't learned metrics.

- Write **directions** telling how to make a cube or any other geometric figure.

- Write a **book jacket** for your math book . . . or an index . . . or a table of contents.

- Write an **advertising brochure** for a resort, camp, cruise, or hotel. Determine what the rate will be for individuals, families, and groups.

Adapted From IF YOU'RE TRYING TO TEACH KIDS HOW TO WRITE, YOU'VE GOT TO HAVE THIS BOOK!
©1995 by Incentive Publications, Inc. Nashville, TN. Used by permission.

Writing Yellow Pages, Rev. Ed.

Social Studies

- Write **announcements** for events that happened in the past.

- Write a **rap rhyme** that will help students learn about the agencies in the U.S. government.

- Write **news flash reports** about an event from world history.

- Write an **invitation** to an event that happened in the past in U.S. history.

- Create a **campaign poster** for a past president or leader of any nation.

- Write the **lyrics** for a theme song for one of the famous revolutions of the past.

- Write a **birth announcement** or **eulogy** for any historical figure.

- Create a **handbook** (illustrated) of the great geographical landforms of the world.

- Compile a **scrapbook** of family history, including a family tree and interesting information about your heritage. Write letters to relatives to gather the information.

- Make a **time line** showing major events and influences in your life or in the life of a current or past public figure.

- Create a **photo essay** on a person or situation in current events.

- Write a **gossip column** from history (telling about figures from the past) as a newspaper back then might have told it.

- Turn a current event or a past event into a **tall tale**.

- Write **travel brochures** . . . for any place . . . here or there . . . now or in the past. Include information about the culture, characteristics, attractions, and geography of the place. Make it enticing so readers would want to visit the place.

- Develop a **flag**, **seal**, **symbol**, **pledge**, and **national anthem** for a new country.

- Write a **tribute** to the Red Cross or any other social organization that has played a part in current or past world events.

- Write **predictions** for the future of any current public figure.

- Create an imaginary (or real) club or organization. Write a **constitution** for your club.

- Choose ten different geographical areas of the world. Write a **weather forecast** that might be typical for each of those ten areas.

- Write a **Guidebook** to Role Expectations. . . describing expectations for behaviors for persons in various roles within various social groups.

- Keep a Cultural Values **Scrapbook**. Find news clippings or pictures or magazine ads that demonstrate particular values held by your culture. (Or, you might include different cultures.). For each piece you put into the scrapbook, write an explanation telling what values are shown by that piece.

Art

Mix art experiences with different kinds of writing. Try these combinations:

- **chants** and sand paintings

- **impressionistic poems** and torn paper mosaics

- **mysteries** and a shadow show, or designs torn from black paper

- **biographies** and portraits

- **color words** or **phrases** and batik or tie-dye

- **monster tales** and squished paint blobs

- **wind poems** and pinwheels

- **haiku** and silk-screens or bamboo painting

- **earth poetry** and rock painting or mud painting

- **scenery descriptions** and wet watercolor paintings

- **lies** or **tall tales** and oversized, exaggerated figures

- **snow poetry** and soap bubble paintings

- **limericks** and vegetable people or cartoons

- **poems** about feelings and wet chalk designs

- **myths** and paper-maché masks or clay-sculpted masks

- **city poems** and skyline paintings

- **autobiographies** or **self-descriptions** and head silhouettes

- **ecology posters** and junk sculptures

- **proverbs** and clay plaques or wooden plaques

- **spooky tales** and black crayon-resists

- **value statements** and totem poles

- **dialogues** and puppets

- **advertisements** and banners

- **epitaphs** and stone-rubbings

- **proverbs** and eye-grabbing posters

- **future predictions** and psychedelic paintings

Adapted From *IF YOU'RE TRYING TO TEACH KIDS HOW TO WRITE, YOU'VE GOTTA HAVE THIS BOOK!*
©1995 by Incentive Publications, Inc. Nashville, TN. Used by permission.

LETTER-WRITING FORMS

BLOCK STYLE

[your street address]   *
[your city, state, and Zip]   *   *HEADING*
[the date]

[addressee's name]
[company's name]   *INSIDE ADDRESS*
[company's street address]
[company's city, state, and Zip]

_____ :   *GREETING/SALUTATION*

_____
_____
_____
_____ .
                                      BODY OF LETTER
_____
_____ .

_____
_____ .

_____ ,   *COMPLIMENTARY CLOSE*

[your handwritten name]   *SIGNATURE*
[your typed name]

* *Do not include if you are using paper with a letterhead on it.*

MODIFIED BLOCK STYLE

HEADING   [your street address]   *
                   [your city, state, and Zip]   *
                   [the date]

[addressee's name]
[company's name]
[company's street address]   *INSIDE ADDRESS*
[company's city, state, and Zip]

_____ :   *GREETING/SALUTATION*

_____
_____
_____
_____ .
                                      BODY OF LETTER
_____
_____ .

_____
_____ .

COMPLIMENTARY CLOSE   _____ ,

SIGNATURE   [your handwritten name]
                          [your typed name]

* *Do not include if you are using paper with a letterhead on it.*

MODIFIED SEMIBLOCK STYLE

HEADING   [your street address]   *
                   [your city, state, and Zip]   *
                   [the date]

[addressee's name]
[company's name]
[company's street address]   *INSIDE ADDRESS*
[company's city, state, and Zip]

_____ :   *GREETING/SALUTATION*

_____
_____
_____
                                      BODY OF LETTER
_____
_____ .

COMPLIMENTARY CLOSE   _____ ,

SIGNATURE   [your handwritten name]
                          [your typed name]

* *Do not include if you are using paper with a letterhead on it.*

FRIENDLY LETTER STYLE

HEADING   [your street address]   *
                   [your city, state, and Zip]   *
                   [the date]

_____ :   *GREETING/SALUTATION*

_____
_____
_____ .
                                      BODY OF LETTER
_____
_____
_____
_____ .

_____ .

COMPLIMENTARY CLOSE   _____ ,

SIGNATURE   [your handwritten name]

* *Do not include if this information is printed or engraved on your stationery.*

PROOFREADERS' MARKS

INSTRUCTION	MARK IN MARGIN	MARK IN TYPE	CORRECTED TYPE
Delete	ℰ	the ~~good~~ word	the word
Insert indicated material	good	the ∧word	the good word
Let it stand	stet	the ~~good~~ word	the good word
Make capital	cap	the word	the Word
Make lower case	lc	⁄The Word	the Word
Set in small capitals	sc	See word.	See WORD.
Set in italic type	ital	The word is word.	The word is *word*.
Set in roman type	rom	the ⟨word⟩	the word
Set in boldface type	bf	the entry word	the entry **word**
Set in lightface type	lf	the entry **word**	the entry word
Transpose	tr	the ⟨word good⟩	the good word
Close up space	⌒	the wo rd	the word
Delete and close up space	ℰ̃	the w ̸ord	the word
Spell out	sp	②words	two words
Insert: space	#	the⁄word	the word
period	⊙	This is the word∧	This is the word.
comma	⋏	words∧words, words	words, words, words
hyphen	⌢=⌢/⌢=⌢	word∧for∧word test	word-for-word test
colon	⊙	the following words∧	the following words:
semicolon	⋏;	Scan words∧skim pages.	Scan words; skim pages.
apostrophe	⋁	John˅s words	John's words
quotation marks	⟨⟨/⟩⟩	the word˅word˅	the word "word"
parentheses	(/)/	the∧word∧word	the word (word)
brackets	[/]/	He read from the Word ∧the Bible∧.	He read from the Word [the Bible].

48

Writing Yellow Pages, Rev. Ed.

INSTRUCTION	MARK IN MARGIN	MARK IN TYPE	CORRECTED TYPE
Insert: en dash	$\frac{1}{N}$	1964∧1972	1964–1972
em dash	$\frac{1}{M}$/ $\frac{1}{M}$/	The dictionary∧how often it is needed∧belongs in every home.	The dictionary—how often it is needed—belongs in every home.
superior type	$\vee$2	$2^\vee = 4$	$2^2 = 4$
inferior type	$\wedge$2	HO∧	H_2O
asterisk	$\vee$*	word$\vee$	word*
dagger	†	a word∧	a word†
double dagger	‡	words and words∧	words and words‡
section symbol	§	∧Book Reviews	§Book Reviews
virgule	/	either∧or	either/or
Start paragraph	¶	"Where is it?"∧"It's on the shelf."	"Where is it?" "It's on the shelf."
Run in	(run in)	The entry word is printed in boldface. The pronunciation follows.	The entry word is printed in boldface. The pronunciation follows.
Turn right side up	⊙	th⊙word	the word
Move left	[	[the word	the word
Move right	]	the] word	the word
Move up	⊓	the⊓word	the word
Move down	⊔	the⊔word	the word
Align	‖	the word the word the word	the word the word the word
Straighten line	=	the word	the word
Wrong font	(wf)	the word	the word
Broken type	X	the word	the word

SPELLING HELPS

The following spelling rules are generalizations and do not occur all of the time; however, they are often true and are valuable spelling aids.

1. Each syllable of a word must contain one sounded *vowel (al li ga tor)*.

2. A vowel is more likely to be pronounced short than long *(bed)*.

3. A vowel at the end of a one-syllable word is usually long *(be)*.

4. The final *e* in a one-syllable word is usually silent *(lake)*.

5. When *i* precedes *gh*, it is usually long *(bright)*.

6. The letter *i* comes before *e* except (1) after *c* or (2) when sounded like *a* (as in *neighbor* or *weigh*).

7. Usually, a doubled consonant or vowel has one sound *(letter, boot)*.

8. When two vowels are together, the first one usually says its own name *(team)*.

9. The *ch* sound is often spelled **tch** *(catch)*.

10. The *j* sound is often spelled **dg** or **dge** *(dredge, smudge)*.

11. The *j* sound may be made by **g** *(giant, garage)*.

12. The *k* sound may be made by **c** or **ck** *(came, stack)*.

13. The *gh* combination is usually silent *(dough, fright)*, but sometimes sounds like **f** *(tough, laugh)*.

14. Sometimes the *gh* combination produces a hard **g** sound *(ghost, ghastly)*.

15. The consonants c and g are soft before *i*, *e,* and *y* *(cinder, gentle, cyst)*; otherwise, they are hard *(go, car)*.

16. The ending **–ance** is spelled **–ence** in some words *(endurance, presence)*.

17. The ending **–ous** may follow an *e* or an *i* *(extraneous, delicious)*.

18. The ending **–tion** (sounds like **shun**) is spelled **–cian**, **–sian**, **–sion**, or **–tian** in some words *(station, physician, Prussian, decision, Dalmatian)*.

19. To pluralize a word that ends with a **y** preceded by a consonant, change the **y** to *i* and add **es** *(cry, cries)*.

20. The common prefixes **en–**, **in–**, and **un–** are not used interchangeably.

Writing Yellow Pages, Rev. Ed.

CAPITALIZATION RULES

Capitalize the first letter in

- the first word of a sentence
- the first word in each line of poetry
- the first and all other important words in the greeting of a letter
- the first word in the closing of a letter
- titles of persons (Mr., Mrs., Ms., Dr.)
- titles of high government officials.

Capitalize

- the word I
- initials
- abbreviations (P.O., R.R., C.O.D., Dr., A.M. and P.M.)
- proper adjectives
- the first, last, and other main words in titles of chapters, stories, poems, reports, songs, books, movies, and radio and television programs
- the first word of each main topic and subtopic in an outline
- the first word in the greeting and closing of a letter

Capitalize proper nouns

- names of all persons
- words like mother, sister, and uncle when used in place of or with names
- names of schools, clubs, organizations, and buildings.
- names of streets, avenues, boulevards, roads, and rural routes
- names of cities, towns, counties, states, countries, and continents
- names of rivers, oceans, and mountains
- names of regions (i.e.: the South)
- names of days, months, holidays, and other special days
- names of businesses and special products
- names of languages, nationalities, and special groups
- names of political parties
- names of government departments
- names for a deity
- names of churches and religious denominations
- names of historical events and documents
- names of airlines, ships, and railroads
- names of magazines and newspapers
- the first word of a heading and a subheading in outlines
- the first word after a strong interjection

RULES FOR PUNCTUATION

A period is used:

- at the end of a declarative sentence.
- at the end of an imperative sentence.
- after numerals and letters in outlines.
- at the end of a business request stated in question form.
- after an abbreviation or an initial.

A question mark is used:

- at the end of an interrogative sentence.
- inside parentheses after a date or statement to show doubt.

An exclamation point is used:

- at the end of an exclamatory sentence.
- after a very strong interjection.
- at the end of an imperative sentence that exclaims.

A comma is used:

- to separate items in a series.
- to separate adjectives of equal value.
- to separate a direct quotation from the rest of a sentence.
- to separate the day of the month from the year.
- to separate the names of a city and a state.
- to separate a name from a title (David Bird, President).
- to set off adjectives in an appositive position.
- to set off introductory words like no and now.
- to set off transitional words however, moreover, and nevertheless.
- to set off a name used in direct address.
- to set off a nonrestrictive adjective clause.
- to set off most words used in apposition.
- after the greeting in a friendly letter.
- after the closing in any letter.
- after a last name preceding a first name.
- after a mild interjection within a sentence.
- after an introductory adverbial clause.
- after an introductory participial phrase.
- before the conjunction in a compound sentence.
- whenever necessary to make meaning clear.

Writing Yellow Pages, Rev. Ed.

An apostrophe is used:
- in contractions.
- to show possession.
- to form plurals of letters, figures, signs, and words.

Quotation marks are used:
- to enclose the exact words of a speaker.
- around titles of short plays, short stories, short poems, chapter titles, and songs.

A colon is used:
- when writing time (6:45).
- to introduce a list.
- after the greeting in a business letter.
- in written plays and in other forms of written dialogue after the name of the character speaking.

A semicolon is used:
- to join independent clauses in a compound sentence when a conjunction is not present.
- to precede a conjunctive adverb (therefore, however, furthermore, etc.) used between the coordinate clauses of a compound sentence.
- in place of a comma when a more distinct pause is desired.

Underlining is used:
- below handwritten or typewritten titles of movies, newspapers, books, magazines, ships, and trains.
- to set off foreign words and phrases which are not yet part of the English language.

A hyphen is used:
- in writing compound numbers.
- to divide a word at the end of a line.
- between parts of a compound adjective preceding a noun.

A dash is used:
- to indicate an abrupt break in thought or structure.
- to indicate a parenthetical or explanatory phrase or clause.
- between numbers in a page reference.

Parentheses are used:
- to enclose material that is supplementary, explanatory, or interpretive.
- to enclose a question mark after a date or statement to show doubt.
- to enclose an author's insertion or comment.

SELECTED GRAMMAR TERMS

Abstract Noun — a noun that names things that do not have a physical substance.
Examples: *compassion, honesty, fear*

Active Voice — a verb that expresses action and can take a direct object.
Example: *I threw the ball.*

Adjective — a word that modifies a noun or a pronoun.
Example: *The white ball.*

Adverb — a word that modifies a verb, an adjective, or another adverb.
Example: *Go slowly.*

Antecedent — the word, phrase, or clause to which a relative pronoun refers.
A pronoun must agree in number with its antecedent.
Example: *Erin gave me her ball.*

Articles — the adjectives *a*, *an*, and *the*.

Auxiliary Verb — a verb that accompanies another verb to show tense, mood, or voice.
Example: *She has gone.*

Clause — a group of words that contains a subject and a predicate, and forms part of a compound or complex sentence.
Example: *After I left, she called.*

Collective Noun — a noun that denotes a collection of persons of things regarded as a unit; usually takes a singular verb.
Example: *The committee chooses its own chairman.*

Common Noun — a noun that indicates any one of a class of persons, places, or things.
Examples: *boy; town; ball.*

Comparative Adjective — an adjective form (ending in -er or adding the word more before the adjective) used when two persons or things are compared.
Example: *This apple is smaller and more delicious than that one.*

Complex Sentence — a sentence containing one independent clause and one or more dependent clauses.
Example: *I went to town to shop, but found that all the stores were closed.*

Compound Sentence — a sentence containing two or more independent clauses joined by a conjunction.
Example: *I called my friend, and we talked for an hour.*

Writing Yellow Pages, Rev. Ed.

Compound-Complex Sentence — a sentence that contanins two or more independent clauses and at least one independent or subordinate clause.
*Example: **When she opened the door, no one was on the porch, and the street was empty, too.***

Compound Subject — a subject of a sentence that has more than one noun in the subject of the sentence

Concrete Noun — a noun that names a physical, visible, or tangible item.
*Example: **airplane.***

Conjunction — a word that connects words, phrases, or clauses.
*Example: **I like toast and jam.***

Coordinating Conjunction — a conjunction used to connect two independent clauses.
*Examples: **He grinned, and I giggled.***

Correlative Conjunction — conjunctions which are used in pairs.
*Example: **Neither Alan nor Amy will go.***

Dependent (or Subordinate) Clause — a clause that functions as a noun, adjective, or adverb within a sentence, but cannot stand alone.
*Examples: **What she said was true.***

Direct Object — the noun, pronoun, or noun phrase in a sentence which receives the action of a transitive verb.
*Example: **I threw the ball.***

Gerund — a verb form ending in -ing, usually used as a noun.
*Example: **Skiing is fun.***

Indefinite Pronoun — a pronoun that does not specify the identity of its object.
*Example: **Anyone can come.***

Independent Clause — a clause that contains at least a subject and a predicate, and is capable of standing alone.
*Example: **I went to the store.***

Indirect Object — the noun, pronoun, or noun phrase named as the one to whom action involving a direct object is done.
*Example: **He gave me the paper.***

Infinitive — a non-inflected verb form usually preceded by to, used as a noun, adjective, or adverb.
*Example: **I myself saw it.***

Interjection — an exclamatory word or phrase.
*Example: **Hey! Look out!***

Intransitive Verb — a verb that does not require an object.
Example: She learns easily.

Linking Verb — a verb that can be followed by an adjective that modifies the subject.
Example: Randy is tall.

Modify — to qualify or limit the meaning of.
Example: very small

Noun — a word that names a person, place or thing.
Examples: girl, city, hat

Paragraph — a distinct division within a written work, that may consist of several sentences, that expresses something relevant to the whole work but is complete within itself.

Passive Voice — a verb which expresses state of being and cannot take a direct object.
Example: He was asked to leave.

Past Tense — a verb form that expresses action or condition that occurred in the past.
Example: Yesterday I went to town.

Personal Pronoun — a pronoun that denotes the speaker, person spoken to, or person spoken about.
Example: You can find it.

Positive Adjective — an adjective form used to assign a quality to the word it modifies.
Example: the fast car

Possessive Pronoun — a pronoun that shows possession.
Example: That car is mine.

Predicate — the portion of a sentence or clause that tells something about the subject, consisting of a verb and possibly including objects, modifiers, and/or verb complements.

Predicate Adjective — an adjective that refers to, describes, or limits the subject of a sentence.
Example: The rock is heavy.

Predicate Nominative — a noun following a form of the verb to be in a sentence which modifies the subject.
Example: She is Alicia.

Preposition — a word that shows relationship (often between verbs and nouns or nouns and nouns) and takes an object.
Example: Put it on the table.

Prepositional Phrase — a group of words in a sentence that includes a preposition and its object, along with any modifiers of the object.
Example: Put it on the first table.

Present Tense — a verb form that expresses current time.
Example: I am here.

Pronoun — a word that takes the place of a noun.
Example: I, you, she, it, he

Proper Noun — a noun that names a particular person, place, or thing, and is capitalized.
Examples: Omaha, Jenny

Reflective Pronoun — a pronoun that ends in -self or -selves; used to point the action back to the subject.
Example: You will hurt yourself.

Relative Pronoun — a pronoun that shows a relationship.
Example: It was he who did it.

Run-On (or Fused) Sentence — a sentence in which two complete sentences are run together with no punctuation to separate them.
Example: I went to the movie I ate some popcorn.

Sentence — a basic unit of language which must contain a subject and a predicate.
Example: I went to the movie.

Subject — a word or phrase in a sentence that is the doer of the action, or receives the action (in passive voice), or which is described; must agree in number with the predicate.
Example: Margaret was there. (Margaret is the subject.)

Subjunctive (or Conditional) Mood — a set of verb forms used to express contingent or hypothetical action, usually introduced by if or that, and always taking the plural form of the verb.
Example: If I were you, I would go.

Superlative Adjective — an adjective form (ending in –est or adding the word most before the adjective) used when three or more things are involved in a comparison.
Example: This is the slowest of all cars.

Tense — the form a verb takes in a particular setting or use.
Example: the present tense is scream, the past tense is screamed.

Transitive — a verb which can take an object within a sentence.
Example: He threw the ball.

Verb — a word that shows action, state of being, or occurrence.
Example: run, is, find

EDITOR'S GUIDE FOR PRIMARY WRITERS

Primary writers should be helped to practice these skills for revising and improving their writing.

_____ Use words that readers can understand

_____ Make sure that the main points are clear

_____ Make sure that the ideas make sense

_____ Add more details to make the points stronger

_____ Add more examples or details to make the writing more interesting

_____ Make sure the ideas are in the correct order

_____ Remove weak or ordinary words; replace them with words that are stronger, more unusual, more colorful, and more specific

_____ Include active words; replace inactive words with active ones

_____ Add more interesting words or phrases (fresh, original)

_____ Rearrange words within a sentence for better sound and flow

_____ Rearrange words within a sentence for more clear meaning

_____ Rearrange sentences or lines for more clear meaning

_____ Get rid of words or ideas that are not needed

_____ Revise beginning sentences to make them more exciting

_____ Make sure endings are interesting

_____ Replace weak titles

_____ Make sure there is a strong, clear beginning, middle, and end

_____ Break up long sentences

_____ Use different kinds of sentences (statements, questions, exclamations, compound sentences)

_____ Use different lengths of sentences

_____ Add some metaphors and similes

_____ Add simple dialogue

_____ Check to see that the writing shows the writer's personality (voice)

_____ Check and correct the spelling

_____ Make sure words are correctly capitalized

_____ Check and correct punctuation

Writing Yellow Pages, Rev. Ed.

EDITOR'S GUIDE FOR OLDER WRITERS

Grades 4-8+

_____ Substitute stronger words (*more colorful, more specific*)

_____ Replace inactive verbs with more active, lively ones

_____ Eliminate repetitive or unnecessary words

_____ Add more interesting words (*fresh, rich, original, energizing*)

_____ Add words or phrases that create a certain mood

_____ Rearrange words within a sentence for meaning

_____ Rearrange words or sentences for smoother flow

_____ Expand sentences to include more detail

_____ Include details that are relevant and rich

_____ Make sure main ideas are well-developed and relevant

_____ Revise to improve clarity and focus

_____ Make sure piece has clear organization

_____ Revise to increase reader appeal

_____ Rearrange sentences for different or clearer meaning

_____ Rearrange sentences for better sequence

_____ Rearrange sentences for more interesting sound

_____ Vary sentence length, structure, and rhythm

_____ Replace ordinary titles with strong, "catchy" titles

_____ Create smashing beginnings

_____ Make memorable endings, with clear closure

_____ Eliminate repetitive or unnecessary ideas

_____ Break up excessively long sentences

_____ Decide if the written piece accomplishes the purpose

_____ Strengthen and vary transitions; make sure they are smooth

_____ Include words and ideas that convince

_____ Add dialogue where it would be effective

_____ Adapt content and form to fit the audience

_____ Include literary techniques that make the writing more interesting or appealing (*for example: personification, onomatopoeia, hyperbole, understatement, exaggeration, foreshadowing, or irony*)

_____ Include figures of speech (*metaphors, similes, idioms, puns*)

_____ Strengthen the writer's voice

_____ Remove bias from piece (*unless called for*)

_____ Revise to strengthen voice (*liveliness, originality, personality, conviction, author involvement, good communication with audience*)

_____ Examine pieces for correct conventions (*punctuation, spelling, capitalization, paragraphing, grammar & usage*)

PRIMARY WRITING PROCESS SCORING GUIDE

TRAIT	SCORE OF 5	SCORE OF 3	SCORE OF 1
IDEAS	• The writing is very clear. • The main ideas stand out well. • Strong details support the main idea. • All details are relevant to the main idea. • Ideas have freshness. • Paper holds reader's attention well.	• The writing is mostly clear. • The main ideas are mostly clear. • Details are used but somewhat limited. • Most details are relevant to the main idea. • Some ideas are fresh. • Paper holds reader's attention somewhat.	• The writing is not very clear. • It is hard to identify main idea. • Details are few or not relevant. • Ideas have little appeal to reader. • No clear idea is developed.
WORD CHOICE	• Writer has used colorful, effective, specific words well to convey ideas. • Words or phrases are fresh or unusual. • Writer has used some figures of speech or words that create images.	• Writer has used some colorful, effective, specific words well to convey ideas. • Sometimes words are used in fresh ways.	• Writer has limited use of colorful, specific, or effective words. • Some words are misused or repetitive. • The words do not express the ideas well.
SENTENCES	• Sentences have natural, pleasing flow. • There is smooth flow between ideas. • Sentences vary in length and structure. • Sentences focus attention on main idea. • The sound and flow of the sentences makes reading enjoyable.	• Most sentences have natural, pleasing flow. • There is smooth flow between most ideas. • Sentences vary somewhat in length and structure. • Sentences convey the main idea, but with some awkwardness. • There is some interruption in fluidity.	• Most sentences are not fluid. • The writing is uneven or awkward. • There is little variety in sentence length or structure. • Some sentences are incomplete or run-on. • Sentence structure inhibits clarity of meaning.

A score of 4 may be given for work that falls between 3 and 5 on any given trait. A score of 2 may be given for work that falls between 1 and 3.

Writing Yellow Pages, Rev. Ed.

PRIMARY WRITING PROCESS SCORING GUIDE

TRAIT	SCORE OF 5	SCORE OF 3	SCORE OF 1
ORDER	• The organization allows main ideas and details to be clear and flow smoothly. • The piece has clear beginning, middle, and end. • The piece has a strong opening, and a compelling conclusion. • Ideas are developed in clear sequence.	• The organization is somewhat weak. • The organization mostly allows main ideas and details to be conveyed. • The piece has a beginning, middle, end. • The piece has an ordinary or somewhat undeveloped opening and/or closing. • The sequence is somewhat confusing.	• Clear organization is lacking. • Organization gets in the way of the conveyance of ideas and details. • The beginning and/or ending are not clear. • Important pieces are missing. • The sequence is confusing.
VOICE	• There is a clear personal stamp on the piece. • The writing engages the audience. • The writing has much passion and originality.	• There is a personal stamp on the piece, but it is not consistent or not strong. • The writing engages the audience some of the time. • The writing shows some passion and originality.	• The writing has no personal stamp. • There is little engagement of the audience. • The writing shows little passion or originality.
CONVENTIONS	• There is clear control of capitalization, punctuation, spelling, and paragraphing. • The main piece needs little editing.	• There is some control of capitalization, punctuation, spelling, and paragraphing. • The main piece needs a fair amount of editing.	• There is poor control of spelling, capitalization, punctuation, and paragraphing. There are many errors. • The main piece needs much editing.

A score of 4 may be given for work that falls between 3 and 5 on any given trait. A score of 2 may be given for work that falls between 1 and 3.

GRADES 4–8+ WRITING PROCESS SCORING GUIDE

TRAIT	SCORE OF 5	SCORE OF 3	SCORE OF 1
CONTENT	• The writing is very clear and focused. • The main ideas and purpose stand out clearly. • Main ideas are well-supported with details and examples. • All details are relevant to the main idea. • The ideas have some freshness and insight. • The ideas fit the purpose and audience well. • The paper is interesting and holds the reader's attention.	• The writing is mostly clear and focused. • The main ideas and purpose are mostly clear. • Details and examples are used but may be somewhat limited or repetitive. • Most details are relevant to the main idea. • Some details may be off the topic. • Some ideas and details are fresh; others are ordinary. • The paper is interesting to some degree. • The ideas and content are less than precisely right for the audience and purpose.	• The writing lacks clarity and focus. • It is hard to identify the main idea. • The purpose of the writing is not evident. • Details are few, not relevant, or repetitive. • Ideas or details have little sparkle or appeal to hold the reader's attention. • The paper has not developed an idea well.
WORD CHOICE	• Writer has used strong, specific, colorful, effective, and varied words. • Words are used well to convey the ideas. • Words are well chosen to fit the content, audience, and purpose. • Writer has chosen fresh, unusual words, and/or has used words/phrases in an unusual way. • Writer has made use of figurative language, and words/phrases that create images.	• Writer has used some specific and effective words. • A good use of colorful, unusual words is attempted, but limited or overdone. • The words succeed at conveying main ideas. • The writer uses words in fresh ways sometimes, but not consistently. • The word choice is mostly suited to the content, audience, and purpose.	• There is a limited use of specific, effective, or colorful words. • Some words chosen are imprecise, misused, or repetitive. • The words do not suit the content, purpose, or audience well. • The words do not succeed at conveying the main ideas.
SENTENCES	• Sentences have a pleasing and natural flow. • When read aloud, sentences and ideas flow along smoothly from one to another. • Transitions between sentences are smooth and natural. • Sentences have varied length, structure, sound, and rhythm. • The structure of sentences focuses reader's attention on the main idea and key details. • The sentence sound and variety make the reading enjoyable. • If the writer uses dialogue, it is used correctly and effectively.	• Most of the sentences have a natural flow. • When read aloud, some sentences have a "less than fluid" sound. • Some or all transitions are awkward or repetitive. • There is some variety in sentence length, structure, sound, and rhythm; but some patterns are repetitive. • The sentences convey the main idea and details, but without much craftsmanship. • If the writer uses dialogue, it is somewhat less than fluid or effective.	• Most sentences are not fluid. • When read aloud, the writing sounds awkward or uneven. Some of the paper is confusing to read. • Transitions are not effective. • There is little variety in sentence length, structure, sound, or rhythm. • There may be incomplete or run-on sentences. • The sentence structure gets in the way of conveying content, purpose, and meaning.

A score of 4 may be given for papers that fall between 3 and 5 on a trait. A score of 2 may be given for papers that fall between 1 and 3.

Writing Yellow Pages, Rev. Ed.

GRADES 4–8+ WRITING PROCESS SCORING GUIDE

TRAIT	SCORE OF 5	SCORE OF 3	SCORE OF 1
ORGANIZATION	• The organization of the piece allows the main ideas and key details to be conveyed well. • The piece has a compelling beginning that catches the attention of the reader. • Ideas are developed in a clear, interesting sequence. • The piece moves along from one idea, sentence, or paragraph to another in a manner that is smooth and useful to develop the meaning. • The piece has a compelling ending that ties up the idea well and leaves the reader feeling pleased.	• Organization is recognizable, but weak or inconsistent in some places. • For the most part, the organization of the piece allows the main ideas and key details to be conveyed. • The structure seems somewhat ordinary, lacking flavor or originality. • The piece has a beginning that is not particularly inviting to the reader or not well-developed. • Some of the sequencing is confusing. • The piece does not always move along smoothly or clearly from one idea, sentence, or paragraph to another. • The piece has a clear ending, but it is somewhat dull or underdeveloped, or does not adequately tie up the piece.	• The piece lacks clear organization. • For the most part, the lack of good organization gets in the way of the conveyance of the main ideas and key details. • The piece does not have a clear beginning or ending. • Ideas are not developed in any clear sequence, or the sequence is distracting. • The piece does not move along smoothly from one sentence or paragraph to another. • Important ideas or details seem to be missing or out of place. • The piece leaves the reader feeling confused.
VOICE	• The writer has left a personal stamp on the piece. A reader knows there is a person behind the writing. • It is clear that the writer knows what audience and purpose he/she is reaching. • The writer engages the audience. • The writer shows passion, commitment, originality, and honesty in conveying the message. • The voice used (level of personal closeness) is appropriate for the purpose of the piece.	• The writer has left a personal stamp on the piece, but this is not as strong or consistent as it might be. The reader is not always sure of the writer's presence. • It is not always clear that the writer knows his/her audience and purpose. • The writer engages the audience some, but not all of the time. • The writer shows some passion, commitment, originality, and honesty in conveying the message, but this is inconsistent.	• The writer has not left any personal stamp on the piece. The writing feels detached. • There is little sense that the writer is speaking to the audience or clearly knows the purpose of the writing. • There is little or no engagement of the audience. • The writer shows little or no passion, commitment, originality, and honesty in conveying the message.
CONVENTIONS	• There is clear control of capitalization, punctuation, spelling, and paragraphing. • There is consistent use of correct grammar and language usage. • The strong use of conventions strengthens the communication of the work's meaning. • The piece needs little editing/revision.	• There is some control of capitalization, punctuation, spelling, and paragraphing. • There is inconsistent use of correct grammar and language usage. • The uneven use of conventions sometimes interferes with the meaning. • The piece needs much editing/revision.	• There is poor control of capitalization, punctuation, spelling, and paragraphing. • There is a lack of correct grammar and language usage. • Poor use of conventions obscures meaning. • There are multiple errors; the piece needs extensive editing/revision.

A score of 4 may be given for papers that fall between 3 and 5 on a trait. A score of 2 may be given for papers that fall between 1 and 3.